North Carolina is full of wonderful towns (especially historic ones!), but there's something extra special about those found in and around our North Carolina mountains. North Carolina mountain towns range in size and shape, but they all come packed with unique attractions and wait with warm, welcoming smiles.

You can easily immerse yourself in local art, browse unique shops, and dig into each place's fantastic food scene. Of course, they can be the perfect base for gorgeous state parks, some of the best hiking trails, and the most beautiful waterfalls in North Carolina.

This book contains photographs and travel advice from our time in the North Carolina mountains and foothills. We hope you fall in love with each of these small towns just like we have.

-Christina & Carl

mountain towns
of *north carolina*

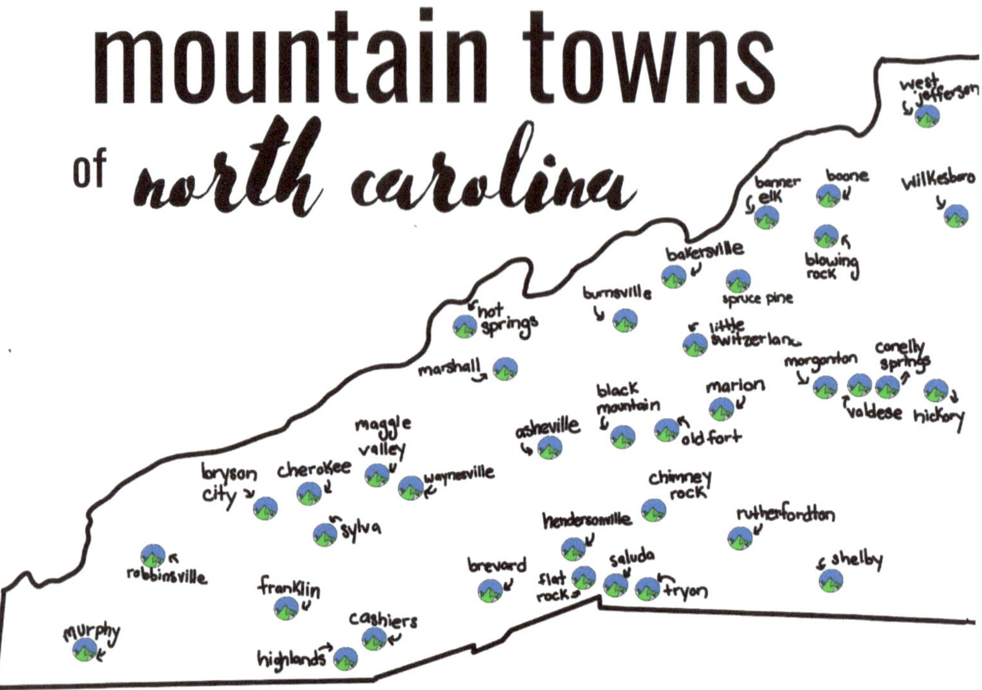

Table of Contents

Note: NC Mountain Towns are alphabetically ordered. Where it makes the most geographical sense, we've also included State Parks sites, Great Smoky Mountains National Park, and the Linville Gorge Wilderness Area. For example, **Grandfather Mountain** follows **Banner Elk**.

Asheville

Asheville is the largest city in the NC mountains and has long been known as one of NC's most incredible mountain towns. We've often used it as a base for nearby hikes and waterfalls. Asheville is also perfect for hopping on the Blue Ridge Parkway or relaxing in luxury at Biltmore Estate or The Omni Grove Park Inn.

Asheville has a fantastic food scene and thriving arts districts, including its world-renowned River Arts District. Make reservations at Curate, walk around downtown, and get a beer at one of the many breweries!

Hikes Near Asheville Checklist

There are almost too many hikes near Asheville to name, with all those surrounding mountains to explore. There may be some overlap with the waterfalls and High Country Hikes checklist, but these 20 hikes are among the best near Asheville that you'll find.

- [ ] Bearwallow Mountain
- [ ] Black Balsam Knob
- [ ] Catawba Falls
- [ ] Crabtree Falls

Craggy Gardens
- [ ] Craggy Gardens Trail
- [ ] Craggy Pinnacle Trail

- [ ] Devil's Courthouse

Dupont State Recreational Forest
- [ ] Hooker Falls, Triple Falls, and High Falls

- [ ] Fryingpan Mountain Lookout Tower
- [ ] Glassy Mountain Trail at the Carl Sandburg Home
- [ ] Graveyard Fields
- [ ] Moore Cove Falls

Mount Mitchell State Park
- [ ] Summit Trail
- [ ] Balsam Nature Trail

- [ ] Mount Pisgah Trail
- [ ] Pink Beds Hike
- [ ] Roaring Fork Creek Falls
- [ ] Skinny Dip Falls
- [ ] Tom's Creek Falls
- [ ] Waterrock Knob

Bakersville

Bakersville is a small mountain town that is also the county seat of Mitchell County and home to the co-op art gallery, Mica Gallery.

Bakersville is also the perfect gateway to Roan Mountain. One of the best views of Mount Mitchell and North Carolina's High Country is from Carvers Gap.

Turn around, and you can look into Tennessee, too.
If you want to visit the area during a specific time of year, June's Rhododendron Festival headlines the annual fun.

Festivals in Western NC

Looking for something to do? Here is a list of annual festivals in Western North Carolina for you to add to your bucket list!

January
First Day Hikes
Blowing Rock Winterfest

February
Asheville Celtic Fest
The Great Outhouses Races (Sapphire)

March
Catawba Valley Pottery & Antiques Festival (Hickory)

April
Block House Steeplechase (Columbus)
Merlefest (Wilkesboro)

May
WNC Bigfoot Festival (Marion)
Yadkin Valley Wine Festival (Elkin)
White Squirrel Weekend (Brevard)

June
Trail Days Festival (Elkin)
Cherry Bounce Festival (Forest City)
Spruce Pine Alien Festival
Boonerang Music & Arts Festival (Boone)
NC Rhododendron Festival (Bakersville)

July
Brushy Mountain Peach Festival (Wilkesboro)
Highland Games (Grandfather Mountain)
Mountain Wildlife Days (Sapphire)

August
NC Mineral and Gem Festival (Spruce Pine)
Mount Mitchell Crafts Fair (Burnsville)
Reevestock Music Festival (Elkin)
Waldensian Festival (Valdese)
Sourwood Festival (Black Mountain)

September
Hickory American Legion Fair (Newton)
NC Apple Festival (Hendersonville)
NC Mountain State Fair (Fletcher)
Historic Morganton Festival
Lake Lure Dance Festival

October
Cashiers Valley Leaf Festival
Tryon International Film Festival
Mush, Music, and Mutts (Shelby)
Woolly Worm Festival (Banner Elk)

Christmas & Holiday Events
Christmas at Biltmore (Asheville)
Polar Express Train Ride (Bryson City)
Tweetsie Christmas (Blowing Rock)
Winterlights at the NC Arboretum (Asheville)

Dates and Locations Subject to Change
For more events, Visit **NCTripping.com**

Banner Elk

Floating high at 3,700 feet in elevation is the High Country town of Banner Elk. Home to the Woolly Worm Festival in October, we can't get enough of this town, the fantastic restaurants and shops here, and its gorgeous surroundings.

Banner Elk is also a popular gateway to Roan Mountain, Grandfather Mountain State Park, and the Mile High Swinging Bridge on the privately-owned Grandfather Mountain attraction. Banner Elk is also surrounded by Beech Mountain and Sugar Mountain, home to two of our best ski resorts.

Grandfather Mountain

When you say "Grandfather Mountain" to someone, you might be referring to just the mountain, the non-profit tourist attraction with the mile-high swinging bridge, or the state park.

Of course, you should visit its mile-high swinging bridge, which requires entering the non-profit tourist attraction side. Inside, you'll also find a fantastic nature museum and trails for all levels of hikers.

On the state park side, trails range from easy to difficult. Grandfather Trail is known as the place where famed botanist Andre Michaux thought he'd reached the highest point in North America.

Western NC State Parks

One of our favorite things to do is to get out and explore our 41 incredible North Carolina State Parks Sites. They include more than 30 established state parks and a handful of recreation and natural areas.

There are 11 NC State Park Sites in Western North Carolina. Have you been to them all?

- ☐ Chimney Rock State Park
- ☐ Crowders Mountain State Park
- ☐ Elk Knob State Park
- ☐ Gorges State Park
- ☐ Grandfather Mountain State Park
- ☐ Lake James State Park
- ☐ Mount Jefferson State Natural Area
- ☐ Mount Mitchell State Park
- ☐ New River State Park
- ☐ South Mountains State Park
- ☐ Stone Mountain State Park

Beech Mountain

Did you know North Carolina's Beech Mountain is the highest town in the Eastern United States? At 5,506 feet, Beech Mountain has incredible views and a great ski resort. You can ride the ski lift to the brewery at the top in the summer months!

Beyond ski season, we love hanging out in this mountain town. Land of Oz (held in September) is one of many great reasons to come here when it's warmer outside. It's truly a unique experience! Tickets go on sale in June and often sell out quickly.

Ski Resorts and Snow Tubing Parks

If you weren't aware, Western North Carolina is a fantastic place for snow tubing and skiing!

Including Beech Mountain, here are the best places to go in the mountains of NC.

Skiing

- [ ] Appalachian Ski Mountain (Blowing Rock)
- [ ] Beech Mountain Resort
- [ ] Cataloochee Ski Area (Maggie Valley)
- [ ] Ski Sapphire Valley
- [ ] Sugar Mountain Resort
- [ ] Wolf Ridge Ski Resort (Mars Hill)

Snow Tubing Parks

- [ ] Beech Mountain Resort
- [ ] Black Bear Snow Tubing (Hendersonville)
- [ ] Highlands Outpost (Scaly Mountain)
- [ ] Jonas Ridge Snow Tubing Park (Newland)
- [ ] Moonshine Mountain Snow Tubing Park (Hendersonville)
- [ ] Sapphire Valley Resort
- [ ] Sugar Mountain Resort
- [ ] Tube World (Maggie Valley)
- [ ] Wolf Ridge Tubing (Mars Hill)
- [ ] Zip N Slip Snow Tubing Park (Mars Hill)

Black Mountain

Just off of I-40, close to Asheville, Black Mountain is a treat of a small town in Western North Carolina! Start by walking around downtown, perusing local shops, and exploring art galleries.

Spend some time at Lake Tomahawk Park, and try not to fall in love with this town. Savor craft brews at Black Mountain Brewing and Lookout Brewing Company.

Enjoy annual events like the Black Mountain Marathon and Sourwood Festival.

Western NC Breweries

Since 2005, the state has seen a boom in high-quality, great craft beer making, creating bucket list-worthy destinations out of breweries. Here are 25 we think you should try, though there are hundreds more deserving of your attention, too!

- [ ] Appalachian Mountain Brewery (Boone)
- [ ] BearWaters Brewing (Maggie Valley. Canton, Waynesville)
- [ ] Blowing Rock Ale House & Brewery (Blowing Rock)
- [ ] Booneshine (Boone)
- [ ] Boojum Brewing Company (Waynesville)
- [ ] Dry Falls Brewing (Hendersonville)
- [ ] Ecusta Brewing Company (Brevard)
- [ ] Fonta Flora (Morganton & Whippoorwill)
- [ ] Green Man Brewery (Asheville)
- [ ] Highland Brewing (Asheville)
- [ ] Hillman Beer (Old Fort, Asheville, Morganton)
- [ ] Hi-Wire Brewing (Asheville)
- [ ] Lazy Hiker Brewing Company (Sylva & Franklin)
- [ ] Lost Province (Boone)
- [ ] Mountain Layers Brewing Company (Bryson City)
- [ ] New Belgium (Asheville)
- [ ] New River Brewing (West Jefferson)
- [ ] Olde Hickory Brewery (Hickory)
- [ ] Oklawaha Brewing Company (Hendersonville)
- [ ] Oskar Blues (Brevard)
- [ ] Sierra Nevada Brewing (Fletcher)
- [ ] Wedge Brewing Co (Asheville)
- [ ] Whistlestop Brewing (Fairview)
- [ ] Whiteside Brewing (Cashiers)

Blowing Rock

We love visiting Blowing Rock for its downtown and the amazing scenery (including hikes and waterfalls) that surrounds it. Visit in spring or fall for ideal weather, or enjoy a quieter winter escape.

The most popular attractions include The Blowing Rock, Chetola Resort, and Tweetsie Railroad. Of course, you can't miss the Glen Burney Trail and Sky Valley Zip Tours. Head into the Blue Ridge Parkway for scenic drives and discover nearby gems like Moses H. Cone Memorial Park, Linn Cove Viaduct, and more!

Blue Ridge Parkway Stops

For this checklist, we'll share 20 awesome stops from North to South and mileposts (MPs) will count up from MP 217 just before Cumberland Knob to MP 469, where the Parkway ends, just around the corner from the Oconaluftee Visitors Center.

- [ ] Cumberland Knob (MP 217.5)
- [ ] Little Glade Mill Pond (MP 230)
- [ ] Doughton Park (MP 238 to 241)
- [ ] EB Jeffress Park (MP 272.5)
- [ ] Moses Cone Memorial Park (MP 294.1)
- [ ] Julian Price Memorial Park (MP 297.1)
- [ ] Rough Ridge (MP 302.8)
- [ ] Linn Cove Viaduct (MP 304.4)
- [ ] Beacon Heights (MP 305.2)
- [ ] Grandfather Mountain Overlook (MP 306.6)
- [ ] Linville Falls (MP 316.4)
- [ ] Bear Den Mountain Resort & Campground (MP 317)
- [ ] Chestoa View (MP 320.8)
- [ ] The Orchard at Altapass (MP 328.3)
- [ ] Little Switzerland (MP 334)
- [ ] Crabtree Falls (MP 339.5)
- [ ] Mount Mitchell State Park (MP 355.3)
- [ ] Glassmine Falls (MP 362)
- [ ] Craggy Gardens (MP 364)
- [ ] Folk Art Center (MP 382)
- [ ] Mount Pisgah (MP 408.6)
- [ ] Fryingpan Mountain Lookout Tower (MP 409.6)
- [ ] Cold Mountain Overlook (MP 411.9)
- [ ] Looking Glass Rock (MP 417)
- [ ] Graveyard Fields (MP 418.8)
- [ ] Black Balsam Knob (MP 420.2)
- [ ] Devil's Courthouse (MP 422.4)
- [ ] Richland Balsam Overlook (MP 431.4)
- [ ] Waterrock Knob (MP 451.2)
- [ ] Southern Terminus (MP 469.1)

Boiling Springs

Gardner Webb University calls Boiling Springs home, and students and parents have a beautiful campus to explore. The town gets its name from the natural spring that feeds into GW's campus.

While driving into Boiling Springs, all the throwback-era general stores and rolling green farmland offer homey vibes that take over long before you park in town. The Broad River Greenway is another great way to get outside and enjoy yourself in Boiling Springs.

Boone

It is no secret that Boone might be our favorite North Carolina mountain town. Every time we visit, we plot our next home to be on a hillside somewhere around here! Home to Appalachian State University (aka App), Boone is a thriving college town with plenty of High Country hikes, delicious and unique restaurants, and breweries.

Arguably, Boone is a four-season destination: hiking and waterfalls in the Spring-Fall and world-class skiing in the Winter.

Elk Knob State Park

Elk Knob State Park near Boone is one of the newer state parks in North Carolina, opening in 2002.

The Summit Trail (1.8 miles) is one of our favorite hikes, leading to beautiful views throughout the year. As long as the conditions aren't too icy, Elk Knob is one of the few hikes near Boone accessible in the winter.

If snow is on the ground, Elk Knob is the only North Carolina state park where you can go cross-country skiing.

Hikes Near Boone Checklist

The High Country is packed with amazing natural beauty (including waterfalls!) and much of it can be witnessed by hiking trails near Boone and Blowing Rock (also, Banner Elk).

Note: You may find some overlap with the "Waterfalls in NC" and "Hikes near Asheville" checklists.

- [ ] Cascades Falls at EB Jeffress Park
- [ ] Crabtree Falls

Elk Knob State Park
- [ ] Summit Trail
- [ ] Elk River Falls
- [ ] Glen Burney Trail

Grandfather Mountain
- [ ] Mile-High Swinging Bridge

Grandfather Mountain State Park
- [ ] Asutsi Trail
- [ ] Profile Trail

Linville Gorge Wilderness Area
- [ ] Hawksbill Mountain Trail
- [ ] Linville Falls
- [ ] Table Rock Summit Trail
- [ ] Wiseman's View

Moses H Cone Memorial Park
- [ ] Bass Lake Trail
- [ ] Flat Top Mountain Fire Tower Trail
- [ ] Otter Falls Trail
- [ ] Roaring Fork Creek Falls

Stone Mountain State Park
- [ ] Stone Mountain Loop

Tanawha Trail
- [ ] Beacon Heights Overlook Trail
- [ ] Boone Fork Trail
- [ ] Rough Ridge Trail

DOWNTOWN
Boone
ELEVATION
3,333
LIVE IT UP

Brevard

Known as the home of the White Squirrel (and annual festival!), downtown Brevard is charming and filled with local shops and the best toy store in North Carolina, O.P. Taylor. With plenty of waterfalls near Brevard, we recommend starting with Looking Glass Falls and keep chasing them until you're tired!

Hot tip: Looking Glass Falls, Moore Cove Falls, and Sliding Rock (pictured below) are all on the same road (US 276) and can all easily be done in a morning!

Waterfalls in North Carolina

With incredible hikes across North Carolina, we've also come across quite a few waterfalls. There are hundreds throughout the state (mostly in Western NC) but here is a checklist of 30 that you must visit!

- ☐ Bridal Veil Falls (Highlands)
- ☐ Bust Your Butt Falls
- ☐ Cascades Falls
- ☐ Catawba Falls
- ☐ Crabtree Falls
- ☐ Dry Falls

Dupont State Recreational Forest
- ☐ High Falls
- ☐ Triple Falls
- ☐ Bridal Veil Falls
- ☐ Elk River Falls
- ☐ French Broad Falls

Graveyard Fields
- ☐ Lower Falls
- ☐ Upper Falls
- ☐ Green Mountain Creek Falls

Hanging Rock State Park
- ☐ Lower Cascade Falls
- ☐ Window Falls
- ☐ Hidden Falls
- ☐ Tory Falls
- ☐ Upper Cascade Falls
- ☐ Key Falls
- ☐ Linville Falls

- ☐ Looking Glass Falls
- ☐ Mingo Falls
- ☐ Moore Cove Falls
- ☐ Rainbow Falls
- ☐ Roaring Fork Falls
- ☐ Setrock Creek Falls
- ☐ Skinny Dip Falls
- ☐ Sliding Rock Falls

Stone Mountain State Park
- ☐ Stone Mountain Falls
- ☐ Widow's Creek Falls
- ☐ Soco Falls
- ☐ Tom's Creek Falls
- ☐ Whitewater Falls

O.P. TAYLOR'S
"The Coolest Toy Store On The Planet!"
O.P. TAYLOR'S BLVD.
N MAIN ST
S BROAD ST
playmobil
OPEN
O.P. TA
BE LOCAL AT HEART
STAY 6FT APART
BREVARD

Bryson City

Bryson City, North Carolina, is a charming mountain town in the Great Smoky Mountains. Downtown Bryson City is a great place to explore, before or after you visit the Great Smoky Mountains National Park.

We love hiking to the Clingmans Dome Observation Tower for panoramic views, and venturing to Deep Creek Trail's waterfalls. Don't miss "The Road to Nowhere" tunnel or outdoor adventures at Fontana Lake and the awesome Nantahala Outdoor Center (NOC).

Great Smoky Mountains National Park

Great Smoky Mountains National Park (GSMNP) is the most visited National Park in the US. Over 900 miles of hiking trails, historic sites, and more await.

Here are a few of our favorite places on the NC side of GSMNP:
- Big Creek Trail (leads to Mouse Creek Falls and more)
- Clingmans Dome Observation Tower (the western terminus of the Mountains to Sea Trail)
- Deep Creek Trail (a three-waterfall hike)
- Mingus Mill (historic grist mill)
- Oconaluftee Visitor Center (info, gift shop, and elk crossing)

Burnsville

Burnsville is one of the best North Carolina mountain towns for exploring the outdoors. It's right on the outskirts of Pisgah National Forest and very close to Mount Mitchell (the tallest mountain east of the Mississippi) and waterfalls, including Crabtree Falls (pictured next page), Setrock Creek Falls, and Roaring Fork Falls.

You'll also encounter a thriving art community through the Toe River Arts and incredible barn quilt trails!

Mount Mitchell State Park

Mount Mitchell State Park manages lands that include the tallest peak east of the Mississippi at 6,684 feet. A 1/4-mile paved accessible trail leads to an observation deck at the top, with panoramic views.

There are plenty of excellent hiking trails within Mount Mitchell State Park, including the Deep Gap Trail, which runs 4.3 miles through Mount Craig, the second-tallest peak.

Riverlife
Royal Crown COLA
RAY'S STORE
HARDWARE
C.C. & GROVER RAY
RAILROAD CROSSING
LOCAL HONEY

Cashiers

Filled with shops, boutiques, and the beautiful Village Green, there is always something to explore in Cashiers. We definitely recommend stopping at Whiteside Brewing for a pint and a burger (or wings!).

There are also some fantastic hikes and waterfalls near Cashiers, including Silver Run Falls and the Panthertown Valley Trail that leads to Schoolhouse Falls.

Gorges State Park

Gorges State Park sits next to Pisgah National Forest (PNF) and is part of a temperate rainforest, receiving more than 80 inches of rain annually. Elevation changes so quickly inside the park that it cools the air that moves, raising the humidity and creating clouds and rain.

This westernmost state park in North Carolina is most notably the access point to the beautiful Rainbow Falls and Turtleback Falls. While this waterfall sits inside PNF, hikers will start their hike from Gorges State Park.

Cherokee

Cherokee is home to the Eastern Band of Cherokee Indians. There are several opportunities to experience the culture and learn the history of these storied Native American people.

Start at the Museum of the Cherokee Indian or the Oconaluftee Indian Village. Many shops are filled with local crafts, and Harrah's Casino is a popular place to play and stay.

Don't forget to visit our favorite waterfalls in Cherokee: Mingo Falls and Soco Falls (pictured above).

Museums in Western North Carolina

Want to learn more about our excellent state and have fun doing it? Look no further than these amazing North Carolina museums. Follow this checklist to the best and most unique in the mountains.

- [ ] American Museum of the House Cat (Sylva)
- [ ] Asheville Art Museum (Asheville)
- [ ] Asheville Museum of Science (Asheville)
- [ ] Asheville Pinball Museum (Asheville)
- [ ] Bennett Classics Antique Auto Museum (Forest City)
- [ ] Biltmore Estate (Asheville)
- [ ] Carl Sandburg Home (Flat Rock)
- [ ] Carson House Museum (Marion)
- [ ] Cradle of Forestry (Pisgah Forest)
- [ ] Earl Scruggs Center (Shelby)
- [ ] Emerald Village & Mining Museum (Little Switzerland)
- [ ] Fly Fishing Museum of the Southern Appalachians (Bryson City)
- [ ] Grandfather Mountain Nature Museum (Linville)
- [ ] Henry River Mill Village (Hickory)
- [ ] Mountain Gateway Museum (Old Fort)
- [ ] Museum of North Carolina Minerals (Spruce Pine)
- [ ] Museum of the Cherokee People (Cherokee)
- [ ] Thomas Wolfe Memorial (Asheville)
- [ ] Scottish Tartans Museum and Heritage Center (Franklin)
- [ ] Smoky Mountains Train Museum (Bryson City)
- [ ] Western NC Nature Center (Asheville)
- [ ] Wheels Through Time Museum (Maggie Valley)

Chimney Rock Village

Chimney Rock Village sits at the entrance of Chimney Rock State Park, a popular North Carolina destination.

While most people come for the famed Chimney Rock attraction and great hiking trails, the Village is a great base that's filled with many historic shops, restaurants, and more.

The 1/3-mile long naturally surfaced Rocky Broad River Walk runs parallel to Main St. It'll connect you to all the shops on the river side of town, with the others just across the street.

Chimney Rock State Park

Just a short day trip from Asheville, the acclaimed Chimney Rock State Park is 8,014 acres and is most known for the iconic 315-foot tall Chimney Rock and the 404-foot Hickory Nut Falls.

Reaching the top of Chimney Rock involves a windy drive and either 500 steps or an elevator ride!

At 404 feet, Hickory Nut Falls is one of North Carolina's tallest waterfalls and can be reached after an easy 0.7-mile hike. Chimney Rock is one of two NC state parks with an admission fee.

Connelly Springs

Connelly Springs is the newest of small towns in North Carolina if you want to be technical about it. They only re-incorporated in 1989, but the buildings and people have been here much longer.

South Mountain Distilling Company (pictured next page), one of our favorite spirit-makers, calls Connelly Springs "home." JD's Smokehouse makes some of the tastiest barbecue we've enjoyed in North Carolina, even if it doesn't style itself as Eastern or Western.

Dillsboro

Dillsboro is an artist community that is one of the coolest North Carolina mountain towns.

With a mix of unique shops and galleries, art festivals, and a charming downtown, this Jackson County mountain town lives and breathes local art.

Dogwood Crafters shares the work of local artisans, and then there's the Dillsboro Chocolate Factory, who'd love to share their fine creations with you.

MASON
ORIGINAL
CHERRY
BOUNCE
MOONSHINE
1846
SOUTH MOUNTAIN DISTILLING CO.
Grain Neutral Spirits with Natural Flavor, Certified Color and Cherries
ORIGINAL
RUTHERFORD COLLEGE · NORTH CAROLINA
30% ALC/VOL · 60 PROOF
750 ML

Elkin

Elkin is one of our favorite small towns for a day trip and a weekend getaway. Whether hiking at Stone Mountain State Park or sipping through the Yadkin Valley, there is always an adventure.

Thanks to some impressive wineries, Elkin gets quite a few visitors. The Surry County Wine Trail features more than a few of the area's best.

Of course, we can't leave out Carter Falls and the Overmountain VIctory Trail, with the latter passing through the town.

REEVES
FRI THE MALPASS BROTHERS
SAT TODD SNIDER W KEVIN GORDON
4/21 MARTHA BASSETT SHOW

Wineries in Western North Carolina

North Carolina has an impressive range of wineries and vineyards, especially in the mountains. Each winery has its flavor and style, and these 25 places are a testament to that diversity.

- [ ] Baker Buffalo Creek Vineyard & Winery (Lawndale)
- [ ] Banner Elk Winery
- [ ] Biltmore Winery (Asheville)
- [ ] Burntshirt Vineyards (Chimney Rock & Hendersonville)
- [ ] Childress Vineyards (Lexington)
- [ ] Curran Alexander Vineyards (Lexington)
- [ ] Divine Llama Vineyards (East Bend)
- [ ] Elkin Creek Vineyard (Elkin)
- [ ] Grandfather Vineyard and Winery (Banner Elk)
- [ ] JOLO Winery and Vineyards (Pilot Mountain)
- [ ] Jones von Drehle Vineyards (Thurmond)
- [ ] Linville Falls Winery
- [ ] McRitchie Winery & Ciderworks (Thurmond)
- [ ] Native Vines Winery (Lexington)
- [ ] Overmountain Vineyards (Tryon)
- [ ] Piccione Vineyards (Ronda)
- [ ] Point Lookout Vineyards (Hendersonville)
- [ ] Raffaldini Vineyards and Winery (Ronda)
- [ ] Rayson Vineyards and Winery (Mocksville)
- [ ] Round Peak Vineyards (Mount Airy)
- [ ] Saint Paul Mountain Vineyards (Hendersonville)
- [ ] Shelton Vineyards (Dobson)
- [ ] Silver Fork Vineyard and Winery (Morganton)
- [ ] Stonefield Cellars (Stokesdale)
- [ ] Thistle Meadow (Laurel Springs)

Flat Rock

Just outside of Hendersonville is the North Carolina mountain town of Flat Rock. Notably, Flat Rock is the home of the Carl Sandburg National Historic Site—the final residence of the famed Pulitzer Prize author. Hike the trails, say hello to the goats, and tour the house all before heading downtown for some beers and yummy food.

Flat Rock is also where you can find one of the most popular places for apple picking in North Carolina—Sky Top Orchard.

Franklin

Franklin is one of two amazing small towns in North Carolina's Macon County that we'll mention. Beer at Lazy Hiker Brewing, gear at Outdoor 76, and a browse (and purchase) at Books Unlimited are a few of the fun things you can explore in downtown Franklin

The town is perfect if you love the outdoors, as it sits near the center of Nantahala National Forest and is a popular Appalachian Trail (AT) rest stop. Wayah Bald Tower is a well-known AT landmark that you can hike or drive to from Franklin.

Appalachian Trail Landmarks in NC

The famed hiking trail runs 2,181 miles through 14 states, including North Carolina. 95.7 miles of it passes through Western NC's mountains and is especially beautiful compared to the rest. Here are some AT landmarks in North Carolina:

- ☐ **Clingmans Dome Observation Tower:** Western terminus of the Mountains-to-Sea Trail and the Appalachian Trail's highest peak.
- ☐ **Fontana Dam:** Cross it like Bill Bryson (and Robert Redford) did in *A Walk in the Woods*.
- ☐ **Lovers Leap:** a 2-mile loop with a gain of 500 feet in elevation, leadir to incredible views.
- ☐ **Max Patch:** a beloved 4,600-foot bald mountain along the NC-Tennessee border with a summit that's just under a mile from the trailhead.
- ☐ **Nantahala Outdoor Center:** an outdoor sports mecca for rafting, kayaking, zip-lining, biking, and hiking!
- ☐ **Roan Mountain:** a series of five mountaintop summits within the Roa Highlands that straddle the North Carolina-Tennessee border.
- ☐ **Wayah Bald Tower:** a historic lookout tower near Franklin that sits a Wayah Bald at 5,342 feet. Drive or hike to it.
- ☐ **Wesser Bald Fire Tower:** a 30-foot tall decommissioned fire tower th you can reach via the Appalachian Trail or a short hike of about 0.7-C miles.

Hendersonville

Hendersonville is one of the largest mountain towns in this book. The Henderson County town is the home of the NC Apple Festival. Known for its high concentration of orchards, apple picking is incredibly popular in this quaint small town.

Hendersonville is an all-around family-friendly destination all year round. Go hiking at the nearby DuPont State Recreational Forest, drive to Jump Off Rock, and find something precious at Elijah Mountain Gem Mine.

Hendersonville is also home to the Appalachian Pinball Museum, a pretty awesome way for young and old to spend an afternoon!

All Nations Trading
Beverly-Hanks & ASSOCIATES
REALTORS

Apple Orchards of North Carolina

- [ ] Apple Hill Orchard (Morganton)
- [ ] Blueberry Thrill Farm (Gibsonville)
- [ ] Carrigan Farms (Mooresville)
- [ ] Coston Farm and Apple House (Hendersonville)
- [ ] Creasman Farms (Hendersonville)
- [ ] Devil Dog Orchard (Reidsville)
- [ ] Grandad's Apples N' Such (Hendersonville)
- [ ] Jeter Mountain Farm Apple Orchard (Hendersonville)
- [ ] Justus Orchard (Hendersonville)
- [ ] Millstone Creek Orchards (Ramseur)
- [ ] Mountain Fresh Orchards (Hendersonville)
- [ ] The Orchard at Altapass (Spruce Pine)
- [ ] Owenby's Apple House & Orchard (Hendersonville)
- [ ] Perry Lowe Orchards (Moravian Falls)
- [ ] Sky Top Orchard (Flat Rock)
- [ ] Stepp's Hillcrest Orchard (Hendersonville)
- [ ] Twisted Apple Orchard (Hendersonville)

Hickory

Hickory, North Carolina, sits at the foot of the Blue Ridge Mountains and along the Catawba River.

The recently revitalized downtown is the perfect base for visitors and locals, new and old. Hickory is a great place to experience arts and culture, starting with the city's Museum of Art and the Catawba Science Center.

Historic landmarks remain, including the Bunker Hill Covered Bridge and the Hickory Motor Speedway.

Waterfall Byway Stops

The North Carolina Waterfall Byway Scenic Drive (in short, Waterfall Byway) refers to the 98-mile stretch of US-64 between Rosman in Transylvania County (near Brevard) and Murphy in far-Western North Carolina.

The North Carolina Department of Transportation designated this scenic road because of the 200-plus waterfalls that surround the byway.

Here are some easy-to-reach stops along the NC Waterfall Byway, from east to west, that you should check out.

- [ ] Panthertown Valley
- [ ] Toxaway Falls
- [ ] Cashiers
- [ ] Highlands
- [ ] Lake Sequoyah
- [ ] Bridal Veil Falls
- [ ] Bust Your Butt Falls
- [ ] Dry Falls
- [ ] Cullasaja Falls
- [ ] Franklin
- [ ] Brasstown
- [ ] Lake Chatuge
- [ ] Murphy

Highlands

The outskirts of Highlands are known for spectacular waterfalls, but this little town is equally beautiful! Spend a luxurious weekend at The Old Edwards Inn and roam the charming shops.

Speaking of waterfalls, view Dry Falls from afar and walk behind it if you'd like. It's one of many falls along the famed Waterfall Byway. That scenic route is another reason we rank Highlands among the best mountain towns in NC!

Hot Springs

Hot Springs is one of the most adorable North Carolina mountain communities, best known for its hot mineral springs. We've used this town as a place to relax but also for hiking the Appalachian Trail, which winds through downtown.

From downtown Hot Springs, you can hike up to Lover's Leap (pictured next page), a 2-mile loop with a gain of 500 feet in elevation. Max Patch Trail is about 45 minutes away from Hot Springs, and an excellent hike for the family to enjoy!

Kings Mountain

Originally known as White Plains due to the amount of mica in the soil, Kings Mountain is named after the famous Revolutionary War battle seven miles away in South Carolina.

When you're in this fantastic Cleveland County town, spend time learning about the area at the Kings Mountain Historical Museum. The Southern Arts Society features rotating exhibits and works from 75 local and regional artists in their gift shop.

Of course, you should get outside at the Gateway Trail, part of the Carolina Thread Trail.

Crowders Mountain State Park

Crowders Mountain State Park in Gaston County, near Kings Mountain and Shelby in Cleveland County.

The trails here are more strenuous but absolutely worthy of your bucket list of NC State Parks hikes. For example, the Pinnacle Trail is four miles round trip and tops 1,705 feet.

On a clear day, you can see the Charlotte skyline from the top, aka the Pinnacle!

Lake Lure

Any time Lake Lure comes up, Christina reminds me that you can have the time of your life here. *Dirty Dancing* fans will know what I'm talking about.

Visit in September and get swept away by the Dirty Dancing Festival. There will be dance, music, arts, and attempts at the famous lake lift.

During the warmer months, enjoy the water via a boat tour or sit back and relax on the beach. We also love the amazing Lake Lure Flowering Bridge that's just off Memorial Highway.

Lakes in Western North Carolina

The state is home to dozens of gorgeous lakes and reservoirs. We love visiting lakes in North Carolina from the mountains to the sea. These are the best lakes in the NC mountains:

- ☐ Bear Lake
- ☐ Fontana Lake
- ☐ Lake Chatuge
- ☐ Lake James
- ☐ Lake Junaluska
- ☐ Lake Lure
- ☐ Lake Santeetlah
- ☐ Lake Toxaway
- ☐ Nantahala Lake
- ☐ W. Kerr Scott Reservoir

Little Switzerland

Little Switzerland is a Blue Ridge Parkway town (MP 334) that is small yet mighty! Here, you'll find a small pocket of stores, a restaurant, and the Switzerland Inn, a mountain resort that is one of our favorite places to stay in North Carolina.

The sweeping views and well-appointed chalets are why we love this place. Many tourists, especially motorcyclists, drive the Diamondback 226 for incredible views and stop for a few nights at The Switzerland Inn or Big Lynn Lodge.

Maggie Valley

Maggie Valley is one of our family vacation spots in the NC mountains. Near many great waterfalls like Soco Falls, we love spending time in this town.

Enjoy creekside beers at BearWaters Brewing, dance at Stompin' Ground, and vroom through the iconic Wheels Through Time motorcycle museum. You'll find vintage motels, motorcyclists, and the best pancakes of your life at Joey's Pancake House!

Marion

Marion is a beautiful town at the base of Mount Mitchell. Downtown Marion features walkable streets, local restaurants, general stores, art galleries, and more.

Tom's Creek Falls is a gorgeous waterfall near Marion, easy to access after a short hike. We also love hiking at the Mount Ida Wilderness Area, just outside downtown.

Visit this town and you'll understand why they say it's where Main Street meets the mountains!

Lake James State Park

Sitting at the base of the most rugged terrain in North Carolina, Lake James State Park (near Marion and Morganton) offers sparkling blue waters perfect for boating.

There are also several awesome hiking, biking, and fishing opportunities here! The accessible fishing pier is a great spot in the Catawba River Area of the park.

You can also ride your bike on loop trails ranging from 1.4 to 6 miles.

Marshall

Madison County seat Marshall sits just north of Asheville and Buncombe County. This mountain town's Main Street has studios, galleries, superb restaurants, and lovely shops.

You can also walk to Blannahassett Island and fish or enjoy views of the French Broad River. Check out the Old Marshall Jail Hotel if you want a unique stay!

While Hot Springs is closer to Max Patch and Lover's Leap, we think Marshall is also a great starting point for those two trails, among other beautiful outdoor spots.

Morganton

Morganton (pictured next page) is another excellent town along I-40 (exit 105) known as the gateway to the Linville Gorge Wilderness Area. On clear days, you can see Table Rock Mountain from downtown Morganton.

This is one of the Gorge's most incredible hikes, and some of our other favorites include Hawksbill Mountain and the Chimneys.

Spend time getting to know downtown, sipping beers at Fonta Flora or shopping at the General Store.

ERTIES
Aqua B
BOUTIQUE
THE
NEWS
HERALD
COFFEE

Linville Gorge

The Linville Gorge Wilderness Area is possibly the happiest place for us to be in the NC mountains. It's home to old-growth forests that have largely remained untouched.

You can camp here, enjoy a picnic, rock climbing, or hop on one of the many hiking trails, including Table Rock Mountain, Linville Falls, and Hawksbill Mountain, but there are many more to explore.

Wiseman's View will give you this fantastic view of the Gorge, in case you were wondering.

South Mountains State Park

South Mountains State Park is also the largest North Carolina state park with 20,871 acres of preserved land. It displays the same rocky features as the nearby Linville Gorge Wilderness Area, but state officials have made it more accessible.

The park's most famous feature is the 80-foot High Shoals Falls (pictured above) which sits along a 2.7-mile loop. Backcountry backpacking camping is available at South Mountains State Park and a strenuous 17-mile mountain biking loop.

Murphy

If you've heard the saying "From Murphy to Manteo," then you might already know that the former is the western end of US-64 in North Carolina. People don't just come here for that bucket list-worthy accomplishment.

You'll love Murphy for its fun downtown and the surrounding NC mountains, water, and trails. Regardless of your religious views, Fields of the Wood (a massive representation of the 10 Commandments) is an interesting place to visit.

Old Fort

If you're driving east on I-40, Old Fort is the last town (exit 73) before you climb toward Black Mountain and Asheville. This town is best known for gold and Catawba Falls. There's a bit of a dispute we won't get into, but Old Fort's Gold Festival typically kicks off each June.

Catawba Falls is a 2.3-mile hike that reopens in 2024, more safely leading to a 100-foot tall waterfall with beautiful cascades. Many people come to this waterfall every year as the trail is an almost entirely flat gravel road.

Robbinsville

Graham County is just above Murphy and Cherokee County along the western edge of NC, home to Robbinsville.

Robbinsville is surrounded by some beautiful places, both natural and manmade. Joyce Kilmer Memorial Forest, the Cherohala Skyway, and Lake Santeetlah are a few nearby destinations.

We suggest a stay at the Historic Tapoco Lodge along the Cheoah River. You might recognize Cheoah Dam nearby from *The Fugitive*, where Harrison Ford's character bravely jumped to escape the law.

Rutherfordton

Rutherfordton is a historic town home to many firsts, including the first US Post Office in Western NC, the first school chartered by the General Assembly, and the first newspaper published in the western foothills and mountain region.

Today, Rutherfordton remains a beautiful downtown to explore. This includes its InterACTIVE Museum (pictured below), a great place to take your kids. Another great place to visit nearby is Forest City, known for its beautiful Christmas lights display, but worth a visit throughout the year!

Christmas Lights Displays in Western NC

Seeing festive displays of Christmas lights in North Carolina is a winter tradition for us. While there are many to name throughout the state, these displays in Western NC are among the best:

- [ ] Candlelight Christmas Evenings at Biltmore (Asheville)
- [ ] Chetola Resort Festival of Lights (Blowing Rock)
- [ ] Dillsboro Lights & Luminaries
- [ ] Forest City
- [ ] JIRDC Lights (Morganton)
- [ ] McAdenville Christmas Town USA
- [ ] Shadrack's Christmas Wonderland at the Tryon Equestrian Center
- [ ] Winter Lights at the North Carolina Arboretum (Asheville)

Saluda

Saluda is a popular spot for rafting and tubing along the Green River. It's a small town that harkens back to simpler times with vintage signs and brick buildings.

Stop in the Pace's General Store (operating since 1899) and Thompson's Grocery Market—North Carolina's oldest grocery store!

Pearson's Falls is also nearby. While it's a rare admission-required waterfall, the area around the 90-foot falls remains well-maintained.

Shelby

More than a few people visit Shelby to learn about Bluegrass legend (and Cleveland County native) Earl Scruggs. Others come to catch a show at the historic Don Gibson Theatre.

The area is also livermush central and you should enjoy it "split and dropped" at the Shelby Cafe.

And of course, we wouldn't leave out Shelby's place in NC Barbecue history. You can explore it further at Red Bridges and Alston Bridges.

Spruce Pine

Spruce Pine is fun to explore, whether driving through the area or staying somewhere like Springmaid Mountain. Stop by Burnette's Country Store while walking around this cute little town.

The Emerald Village near Little Switzerland complex hosts 12 mines for gem and gold panning seven days a week from spring through fall. There's also a cool museum to walk through here.

Spruce Pine is an excellent spot throughout the year, but two events here are cool—the NC Mineral and Gem Festival in August and the Spruce Pine Alien Festival in June.

Sylva

Sylva (pictured next page) is an adorable small town bustling with incredible restaurants and shops. And if you're into beautiful historic buildings, check out the Jackson County Public Library. A nice view of downtown awaits from up there.

Fly fishing is a popular thing to do in Sylva as it is home to the only fly fishing trail in the United States.

Visitors to Sylva will love the natural surroundings, including spots like Pinnacle Park and Wolf Creek Lake. Stick around for fun at the American Museum of the House Cat.

Tryon

Tryon is known for a lot, but its International Equestrian Center is probably the area's biggest name. The Fine Arts Center hosts performances and has collaborated with artists for many years.

Tryon is also the birthplace of the famous musician Nina Simone (Eunice Kathleen Waymon). Nina Simone Plaza in downtown Tryon commemorates this legend's contributions to the music world.

Speaking of downtown, walk around and fall in love with all the shops and restaurants that line Trade Street.

Valdese

We love its downtown and recommend you stop by when driving along I-40 or if you're near Burke County. And don't miss Myra's for a classic burger and ice cream!

McGalliard Falls is another reason you should visit Valdese. It's on the outskirts of town but where you'll find a 40-foot waterfall joining a recreated grist mill. It's just a short walk from the parking lot, too.

Waynesville

Waynesville is the largest town west of Asheville, home to fun on Main Street and around Frog Level. You'll also find the Museum of North Carolina Handicrafts in Waynesville, typically open from May to October.

Waynesville is the largest town in Haywood County, home to adorable shops, amazing restaurants, and surrounded by beautiful outdoor scenery. You'll enjoy walking on its brick sidewalks while admiring the town's historic buildings.

West Jefferson

West Jefferson is a lovely Ashe County town, sitting in the shadows of Mount Jefferson and Paddy Mountain. There's a lovely arts district here, West Jefferson Park to stroll around, and farmer's market that sells locally produced food that includes Ashe County cheese!

New River State Park is also nearby in Ashe County. Don't pay attention to the name, as this is one of the oldest rivers in the US.

Mount Jefferson

You can see Mount Jefferson from the Blue Ridge Parkway, but visit Mount Jefferson State Natural Area (pictured next page) and look down at West Jefferson and its Ashe County surroundings.

You can drive to Mount Jefferson's summit and enjoy beautiful views of its surroundings. But, first, of course, you should hop on one of the park's five fairly short yet difficult hiking trails.

The kid-friendly TRACK trail (1.1 miles) runs from the summit to Luther Rock. From Luther Rock, you can see the New River to the east on clear days.

New River State Park

New River State Park in Ashe County (near Mount Jefferson) features excellent water sports and wildlife viewing opportunities.

There are four access points to this North Carolina state park, but Wayoner Road and US-221 seem to be the most active.

The natural canoe trail at New River State Park is perfect for beginners as the water is shallow and slow. If you do not have your own canoe, Zaloo's is a local company that covers rentals and shuttles.

Where the
Mountains Begin!
Wilkesboro, NC

Special Thanks, in no particular order, go out to the following amazing people:

To the authors of books about North Carolina (William Powell on the history and culture end and Jason Frye on the Travel side) and *Our State Magazine*, thank you for inspiring us to come up with our take on places to go. Also, thanks to Jeremy Jones for design inspiration.

To the Avett Brothers, thank you for continuing to power Carl through many writing sessions, road trips, and challenging times. We look forward to interviewing you someday and learning about your favorite barbecue joints near Concord.

To our friends and colleagues who've cheered us on, we owe you big time! Thanks to Cindy Whitt for providing amazing final edits before publishing this book. Also, a big thank you to Dana Cassell, Aleena Islam, and Caleb Pasiuk for everything you do to keep our website moving.

Those who work in local tourism and PR also deserve a "thank you" for introducing us to the wonderful people in your communities. We've enjoyed working with so many of you. Still, we would also like to give a special shoutout to Jenny Bell, Suzanne Brown, Katherine Christie, Salem Clarke, Craig Distl, Susan Dosier, Veda Gilbert, and Thomas Salley.

To the owners, chefs, managers, and employees who work so hard to keep our state full of amazing locally-owned businesses. Thank you. We will always support you, no matter what.

To the people of NC, thank you for being so kind, welcoming, and proud of where you live.

Finally and most importantly, to you, our reader, thank you for supporting us and keeping us in check. We know you've got our backs.

About the Authors

Carl Hedinger and Christina Riley are the founders of NC Tripping. We started as a website and social media page to highlight local businesses and destinations and inspire travel around North Carolina.

With a love for barbecue, beer, hiking, and small towns, we travel with our young daughter and even younger son and share our adventures at NCTripping.com and @NCTripping on Social Media.

We provide original photography and videos and have a loyal following that appreciates originality and authenticity.